In Winter

by Jane Belk Moncure
illustrated by
Marie Claude Monchaux

Library of Congress Cataloging in Publication Data

Moncure, Jane Belk.
  Winter.

  Summary: Fifteen poems celebrate the snow,
hibernating animals, icicles, and other signs of
winter.
  1. Winter—Juvenile poetry.   2. Children's
poetry, American.   [1. Winter—Poetry.   2. American
poetry]   I. Monchaux, Marie Claude, ill.   II. Title.
PS3563.O517W47   1985   811'.54   85-11663
ISBN 0-89565-330-3

Abdo & Daughters

In Winter

It's that snowy, blowy
time of year
when jingle bells tell us
WINTER IS HERE!

Winter Surprise

I didn't hear a sound.
I didn't see it fall.
I didn't even know
   it was coming at all.
But the first thing I saw
   when I opened my eyes,
   was a winter's night,
      snowy white,
         snowflake
            surprise!

Hiding Places

Where does a chipmunk go
   when it snows?
Where does a turtle stay?
Where is the home for the
   frog or the toad,
      when winter is on its way?
It might be a hiding place
   high in a tree,
      or down in a snuggly hole.
But each will rest
   in a nice warm den,
   'til the warm spring sun,
   wakes it up again.

If ...

If I were a bear,
   I would never hear,
   "Please put on your
   snowsuit, dear."
I would never wear mittens,
   or boots, or a cap!
But Mom says a bear takes a
   long winter nap!
So I guess I won't be a
   bear today.
I'll just put on my boots
   and hop out to play.

Peepholes

My boots make peepholes
  in the snow.
I can see the grass
  way down below.
I walk across the yard
  and then . . .
    follow the peepholes
    home again.

A Giant's Slide

I pretend the hill
  is a giant's slide.
And while he is sleeping,
  I take a ride.
Down I go without a spill!
Then, I climb
  the slippery, sliding-board
    hill.

A Snowman

If I were a snowman,
I would stay
frozen stiff on a winter day.
An icy statue
I would be . . .
  until the sunshine
    melted me.

Icicles

I think icicles are very nice.
I like ice a lot . . .
But, I wish it
  would stay . . .
    'til a summer day
     when I get
      oh, so hot!

Snow Shadow

I took a nap in the snow
   one day.
Just for a minute I stayed
   that way.
When I jumped up,
   guess what I found?
My snow shadow sleeping
   on the ground!

Winter Colors

Winter is white
   with snow and ice,
   glistening in
   the bright sunlight.
Winter is red
   with Santa Claus suits,
   Christmas stockings, and
   red snowboots.
Winter is holly-and-
   Christmas-tree green
   and all the colors
   in between —
   when holiday lights shine
   everywhere,
   and tiny snowflakes
   fill the air.

Candles

Candles make no sound
  at all,
  as they glow brightly
  in the hall.
If they could whisper,
  they would say,
"Just watch us turn
  the night to day."

Outside, Inside

Outside, there's an igloo
   in the snow.
Inside, there's a fire,
   and warm cocoa.
There are gingerbread cookies
   just for me . . .
   and secret boxes
   under the tree!

Caring

Hi! Little chickadee.
Don't fly away.
Come, see your Christmas tree
   today.
Please stay, Mr. Squirrel.
I have something for you,
   and for the bluejay,
   and the rabbit too.
There are peanut-butter pinecones,
   full of seeds for you to eat,
   and cornbread balls,
   with raisins,
      for a very special treat.

Mittens

There were three little girls
   in the family,
   so Santa Claus brought them
   a mitten tree . . .
      with red mittens,
      green mittens,
      and brightest blue,
   with caps and scarves to
      match them too.
On Christmas morning,
   in the cold, snowy weather,
   they wore their new mittens
      as they skated together.

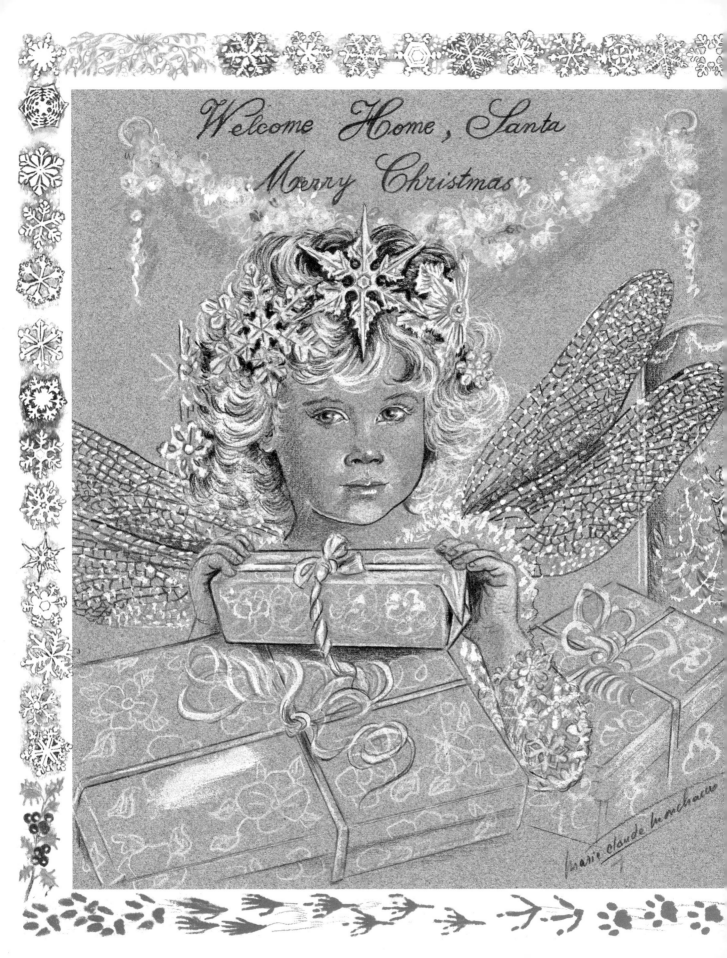

Welcome Home, Santa
Merry Christmas

Santa's Surprise

Does Santa hang a stocking?
Does he have a Christmas Tree?
Who brings his gifts on Christmas Eve
    when he's busy as can be?
Daddy says snowflake fairies come
    when Santa's far away.
They bring him gifts and decorate
    his tree for Christmas day.